NBA
Records

Illustrations by Sanford Hoffman
Compiled by Jeanne Tang

Sterling Publishing Co., Inc. New York

10 9 8 7 6 5 4 3 2 1

Published by Sterling Publishing Company, Inc.
387 Park Avenue South, New York, N.Y. 10016
© 1996 by NBA Properties, Inc.
Distributed in Canada by Sterling Publishing
%o Canadian Manda Group, One Atlantic Avenue, Suite 105
Toronto, Ontario, Canada M6K 3E7
Distributed in Great Britain and Europe by Cassell PLC
Wellington House, 125 Strand, London WC2R 0BB, England
Distributed in Australia by Capricorn Link (Australia) Pty Ltd.
P.O. Box 6651, Baulkham Hills, Business Centre, NSW 2153, Australia
Printed and bound in France

Sterling ISBN 0-8069-4852-3

How to Use the BipPen

The BipPen must be held straight to point to a black dot.

Point to the black dot.

●

A continuous sound (beeeep) and a red light mean that you've chosen the wrong answer.

Point to the black dot.

●

A discontinuous sound (beep beep beep) and a green light mean that you've chosen the right answer.

Keep your BipPen for other books..

Winning an NBA championship is a great achievement. That is why it is difficult for a team to win several in a row. However, there is one team in the NBA that won an extraordinary eight straight championships from 1959 to 1966. Which team was it?

Los Angeles Lakers ●
New York Knicks ■
Boston Celtics ▲

Blocked shots records have only been compiled since 1973-74. Today, blocked shots is one of the major statistical categories the NBA tracks. Can you name the player who holds the career record for blocks?

Mark Eaton ●
Kareem Abdul-Jabbar ■
Manute Bol ▲

NBA teams play a tough 82-game regular season schedule. They didn't always play that many. In the league's first season, teams only played 60 games. The NBA slowly added more games in succeeding seasons before settling at 82 games in 1967. Can you name the team that holds the record (69-13) for the most victories in a single season?

Chicago Bulls
Los Angeles Lakers
Philadelphia 76ers

An assist is a pass that leads directly to a score and John Stockton is one of the best at passing the ball in history. He holds the record for the most assists all-time and the most assists in a single season. But Stockton does not have the record for the most assists in a single game. Do you know who does?

Scott Skiles ●
Magic Johnson ■
Bob Cousy ▲

Michael Jordan has won seven consecutive scoring titles, a feat he shares with one other player. Can you name that player?

George Gervin
Dominique Wilkins
Wilt Chamberlain

The 1971-72 Los Angeles Lakers have the record for winning the most number of games in a row. Do you know how many games they won on that record-breaking streak?

41
33
24

On the other side of the coin, the 1972-73 Philadelphia 76ers and the 1993-94 Dallas Mavericks share the record for the most consecutive games lost in one season. How many did they lose in a row?

20 ●
28 ■
15 ▲

Since 1966, the Houston Rockets have had the first overall pick in the NBA Draft four times—more than any other team. Houston drafted Elvin Hayes in 1968, John Lucas in 1976 and Hakeem Olajuwon in 1984. Who did they draft first in 1983?

Rodney McCray ●
Ralph Sampson ■
Craig Ehlo ▲

A regulation NBA game is 48 minutes in duration. If the score is tied at the final buzzer, the teams play additional five-minute overtime periods to determine the winner. The 1990-91 Philadelphia 76ers needed that extra time often; they were involved in a record number of overtime games that season. How many OT games did they play?

14 ●
10 ■
18 ▲

Which franchise has won the most NBA Championships—16?

Chicago Bulls ●
Los Angeles Lakers ■
Boston Celtics ▲

Kareem Abdul-Jabbar has scored more points than anyone else in NBA history with 38,387. Do you know who is in second place in the record books with 31,419?

Moses Malone ●
Wilt Chamberlain ■
Oscar Robertson ▲

Basketball is a physically demanding sport and it takes a real "iron man" to play in every game. Who holds the record for the most consecutive games played—906?

Randy Smith
Dolph Schayes
A.C. Green

Everyone knows that Wilt Chamberlain holds many scoring records, but it is not widely known that Wilt also holds the all-time mark for the most assists in a game by a center. What is that record-setting number?

15
21
27

Some fans of the NBA might have the opinion that there are too many fouls called in a game. But in the early days of the league, far more fouls were called. In a game involving the Anderson Packers and the Syracuse Nationals (now the Philadelphia 76ers), November 24, 1949, a record number of fouls were committed. Can you guess that number?

66 ●
50 ■
78 ▲

15

There has been only one player ever to lead the league in scoring and assists in the same season. This player averaged 33.9 points and 11.4 assists in 1972-73. Can you name this unique player?

Magic Johnson ●
Oscar Robertson ■
Nate "Tiny" Archibald ▲

16

Lenny Wilkens became the all-time winningest coach in NBA history during the 1994-95 NBA season. Whose record did he surpass?

Red Auerbach ●
Cotton Fitzsimmons ■
Jack Ramsay ▲

In 1993-94, Patrick Ewing shared a distinction with one other player for winning the most opening taps. They each won 56 taps for a 71 percent success rate. Who was the other player?

David Robinson ●
Dikembe Mutombo ■
Shaquille O'Neal ▲

The Boston Celtics have had the most players named the NBA Most Valuable Player with four. These four players have won 10 awards collectively—the most from any one team. Bob Cousy, Bill Russell and Larry Bird are three. Who is the fourth?

John Havlicek ●
Dave Cowens ■
Kevin McHale ▲

From 1965 to 1980, a center won the NBA MVP award every season. Can you name the forward who broke the dominance of the centers by winning the 1981 MVP?

Julius Erving
Adrian Dantley
Larry Bird

There is only one player in the history of the NBA who has won three consecutive NBA Finals Most Valuable Player awards. Do you know who that player is?

Kareem Abdul-Jabbar
Isiah Thomas
Michael Jordan

Rebounding is one of the keys to winning ballgames. During the Celtics' great stretch of winning eight championships in a row, they often led the league in rebounding. Of course, it helped greatly that one of the best rebounders ever, Bill Russell, played on those teams. Do you remember who the Celtics' opponent was when the team set the all-time record of 109 rebounds in a single game, December 24, 1960?

Detroit Pistons ●
Minneapolis Lakers ■
St. Louis Hawks ▲

Who scored 61 points—the most ever—in one game of the NBA Finals?

Michael Jordan
Elgin Baylor
Rick Barry

According to the season-opening rosters for the 1994-95 season, this club was the tallest team in the league, boasting a league-high four 7-footers. The average height of this team was 6-9. Can you guess which team?

Orlando Magic
Chicago Bulls
Seattle SuperSonics

In the same survey of opening day rosters, do you know which team was the shortest in the NBA with an average height of 6-5? Hint: This team has Muggsy Bogues, the shortest player in NBA history at 5-3, playing for it.

Charlotte Hornets
Utah Jazz ■
Sacramento Kings ▲

Which team was the lightest in 1994-95 with an average weight of 213.58 pounds?

Dallas Mavericks
Philadelphia 76ers ■
Cleveland Cavaliers ▲

Winning on the road during the regular season is difficult, but winning on the road during the playoffs is especially tough. That's because teams know that they must win at home to have success in the postseason. Which team set a record with nine playoff road wins in 1995?

Houston Rockets ●
Washington Bullets ■
Chicago Bulls ▲

The New York Knicks played a record number of playoff games in 1993-94 only to lose the NBA Championship to the Houston Rockets in the 1994 Finals. How many playoff games did New York play?

14 ●
25 ■
26 ▲

Who holds the rookie scoring record for the most points in one game of the NBA Finals? This player poured in 42 points.

Magic Johnson ●
Tommy Heinsohn ■
Elgin Baylor ▲

The average weight of NBA players went down to 221.5 pounds for the 1994-95 season from a record 221.68 pounds the season before. Which team was the heaviest with an average player weight of 234.71 pounds? This team had four players weighing more than 250 pounds.

New Jersey Nets ●
Seattle SuperSonics ■
Phoenix Suns ▲

In 1984, Magic Johnson, one of the most talented passers in history and second all-time in assists, led the league in that category. However, an assist record was set that season which did not involve Johnson. The record of 93 assists in one game by both teams was set in a triple-overtime game, December 13, 1983. The Detroit Pistons had 47 assists in that game. Who was their opponent with 46 assists?

Denver Nuggets ●
Boston Celtics ■
Milwaukee Bucks ▲

Since the three-point shot was adopted by the NBA for the 1979-80 season, only three players had attained 1,000 career threes by the end of the 1994-95 season. Dale Ellis and Reggie Miller were the first two to reach that milestone. Who joined them as the third?

Terry Porter ●
Danny Ainge ■
Chuck Person ▲

Not known as one of the league's better free throw shooters in his day, this player surprisingly has the record for the most free throws made in a game with 28. Who was that player?

Wilt Chamberlain ●
Jerome Lane ■
George Mikan ▲

Rookies, because of their inexperience, often don't get to play many minutes. But occasionally a truly great player comes along who contributes immediately. Players like Kareem Abdul-Jabbar or Shaquille O'Neal come to mind. But neither of these players holds the record for most minutes played by a rookie in a season. Who owns that record?

Chris Webber ●
Charles Barkley ■
Elvin Hayes ▲

This player is known as one of the best free throw shooters ever. He holds the record for the highest free throw percentage in a season. During the 1980-81 season, he hit from the charity stripe 95.8% of the time. Do you know his name?

Rick Barry

Calvin Murphy

Chris Mullin

35

Can you guess which was the most popular number worn by NBA players in the 1994-95 season? This number was sported by 17 players. Hint: Charles Barkley and Hakeem Olajuwon wear this number.

32

34

3

Speaking of numbers... As a tribute to a player's excellence and service to the team, a ballclub will often retire that player's number so that no other player can wear that number again while playing for that club. Which team has had the most numbers retired with 19 numbers out of circulation?

Boston Celtics
New York Knicks ■
Golden State Warriors ▲

True or False: In an historic game March 2, 1962 at Hershey, PA, Wilt Chamberlain of the Philadelphia Warriors scored an all-time high of 100 points in a 169-147 victory over the New York Knickerbockers.

True ●
False ■

The NBA Playoffs are intense. Some players rise to the challenge and revel in the pressure while others shrink from the limelight. This player is certainly not one to succumb to pressure. He scored 63 points—the most ever—in a playoff game. Who was that player?

Clyde Drexler ●
Michael Jordan ■
Charles Barkley ▲

At the conclusion of the 1993-94 season, how many different franchises had won NBA Championships?

15 ●
27 ■
32 ▲

Since the NBA Finals MVP award was instituted for the 1969 Finals, there has only been one player who won the award but not the championship. That strange occurrence happened the first year of the award in 1969. Who is the only man to win the Finals MVP without winning the NBA Finals that year?

Jerry West
Wilt Chamberlain
Elgin Baylor

Which NBA head coach owns the record for most playoff victories?

Phil Jackson
Lenny Wilkens ■
Pat Riley ▲

True or false: When we say that Kareem Abdul-Jabbar played 1,560 games, more games than anyone else, this number includes both regular season and playoff games.

True, the all-time records take into account every game played. ●
False, regular season records and playoff records are kept separately. ■

No team in NBA history has ever come back from a 3-0 deficit in a best-of-7 format to win a playoff series. In fact, only five teams have been able to wipe out 3-1 deficits. The Houston Rockets, Los Angeles Lakers and Washington Bullets each did it once, while the Boston Celtics came back from the brink twice. Interestingly, the Celts defeated the same team both times. Which team was that?

Los Angeles Lakers ●
Philadelphia 76ers ■
Milwaukee Bucks ▲

Here is a record of futility that no player shoots for. Do you know who holds the record for most shot attempts (17) in a game without making any?

Tim Hardaway
Otis Thorpe
Mark Eaton

45

Who holds the record for most seasons played in the NBA, 20, a record that Robert Parrish will tie if he plays in 1995–96?

Moses Malone
Bill Cartwright
Kareem Abdul-Jabbar

46

When a player commits six fouls, he is disqualified from the game. Who owns the dubious record for the most disqualifications all-time?

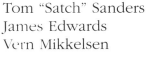

Tom "Satch" Sanders
James Edwards
Vern Mikkelsen

Three teams have won every Finals they have ever appeared in. Two of the teams are the defunct Baltimore Bullets and the Rochester Royals (now the Sacramento Kings). What is the only other perfect team?

Chicago Bulls
Seattle SuperSonics
Detroit Pistons

The NBA All-Star Game is the annual showcase of the league's best players in a contest pitting the Eastern Conference against the Western Conference. Yes or no: The East All-Stars defeated the West in the first-ever All-Star Game.

Yes
No

49

Following the 1995 NBA All-Star Game, which conference had 28 wins against 17 defeats?

Eastern Conference
Western Conference

50

Considering how many years he played in the NBA, it is not surprising that this player has played in more All-Star Games than any other. Do you know who this 18-time All-Star is?

Bob Cousy
Oscar Robertson
Kareem Abdul-Jabbar

51

The Schick Rookie Game was added to the All-Star Saturday slate in 1994. Do you remember who won the first-ever Rookie Game MVP award?

Anfernee Hardaway
Chris Webber
Isaiah Rider

52

Since he holds so many scoring records, no one should be astonished that Wilt Chamberlain also has the record for most points scored in an All-Star Game. How many did Wilt score to set the record?

56 ●
42 ■
35 ▲

The AT&T Long Distance Shootout has been a part of the NBA All-Star Weekend since 1986. Larry Bird and one other player have won the Shootout crown three times. Who shares this record with Larry?

Mark Price
Dale Ellis
Craig Hodges ▲

Three players have won the NBA Slam-Dunk Championship twice. But only one has won it back to back. Who did it?

Dominique Wilkins
Michael Jordan
Harold Miner ▲

When Grant Hill started in the 1995 All-Star Game, he became only the 15th rookie ever to start in the midseason classic. He joined Shaquille O'Neal as the only two rookies to be voted onto the starting squads so far in the 1990s. Two other rookies in the past not only started the game, but won the All-Star MVP award. Wilt Chamberlain did it in 1960, and the very next year another rookie equaled Wilt's accomplishment. Who won the All-Star MVP award in 1961?

Oscar Robertson ●
Wayne Embry ■
Gene Shue ▲

Individual player turnovers have been compiled as an official statistic by the NBA since the 1977-78 season. Who committed the most turnovers in his career?

Moses Malone
Artis Gilmore ●
Reggie Theus ■
▲

57

The now-defunct Baltimore Bullets did not win one away game during the 1953-54 season. They were a miserable 0-20 on the road. Which team in recent years challenged Baltimore's record by winning only one away game in a season?

Dallas Mavericks ●
Minnesota Timberwolves ■
Sacramento Kings ▲

58

Then-rookie David Robinson helped the 1989-90 San Antonio Spurs to the biggest one-season turnaround in league history. The year before, the Spurs won just 21 games. With Robinson, they won the Midwest Division title. How many more games did Robinson help the Spurs win?

25 ●
35 ■
40 ▲

Which team holds the record for most
steals in a season?

Phoenix Suns
Seattle SuperSonics
Golden State Warriors

Which player owns the record for most
steals in a season? This player snat-
ched 301 balls in one year.

Micheal Ray Richardson
Nate McMillan
Alvin Robertson

The 1971-72 Los Angeles Lakers not only hold the record for the most victories in a season with their remarkable 69-13 record, but they also set the record for the highest winning percentage in road games that year. How many away victories did the Lakers have?

40 ●
31 ■
37 ▲

Since 1966, only five guards have been selected with the No. 1 overall pick in the NBA Draft. Which of the following guards was drafted first overall?

Magic Johnson ●
Isiah Thomas ■
Michael Jordan ▲

The NBA Draft Lottery was introduced in 1984 to determine the order of selection at the start of the NBA Draft. The Lottery only involves teams that did not make it into postseason play, and presently only determines the first three selections. After the top picks are determined, the rest of the clubs pick in inverse order of their regular season record, so the team with the best record in the league picks last. Since 1984, one team has won the Lottery in consecutive years. Which lucky team got to pick first two years in a row?

Houston Rockets
Orlando Magic
Charlotte Hornets

64

The Detroit Pistons participated in the highest-scoring game in NBA history back in 1983. They defeated this opponent, 186-184, in a triple overtime game:

Denver Nuggets
Los Angeles Lakers
Chicago Bulls

65

The Pistons were also involved in the lowest-scoring game in NBA history. Playing as the Fort Wayne Pistons in 1950, the team defeated this opponent 19-18:

Syracuse Nationals
Minneapolis Lakers
Tri-Cities Blackhawks

Which team holds the record for the most offensive rebounds in a season?

Boston Celtics
Houston Rockets
Denver Nuggets

Which team holds the record for the most defensive rebounds in a season?

Denver Nuggets
Boston Celtics
Orlando Magic

Which team once went 40-1 to set the NBA record for most wins at home during a regular season?

Los Angeles Lakers
Chicago Bulls
Boston Celtics

True or false: The NBA All-Rookie Team is similar to other All-NBA teams in that the squad comprises two guards, two forwards and one center.

True, it is chosen by position like the other award teams.

False, members of the All-Rookie Team are chosen regardless of position.

There were 304 points scored in the highest-scoring playoff game ever, a double overtime victory, 153-151, for the Portland Trail Blazers. Who was the Blazers' opponent in that game?

Phoenix Suns
San Antonio Spurs ■
Seattle SuperSonics ▲

Since the Boston Garden played host to its last basketball game at the end of the 1994-95 season, this player's record of 62 points in that building will now stand for all time:

Wilt Chamberlain ●
Larry Bird ■
Dominique Wilkins ▲

When the Chicago Stadium closed its doors for good at the end of the 1993-94 season, Michael Jordan owned four of the five top scoring performances in the arena. Jordan, however, did not hold the top spot. This player scored 68 points to set the record during the 1967-68 season:

Dave Bing ●
Wilt Chamberlain ■
Jerry West ▲

The average age of players in the league in 1994-95 was 28. Who was the oldest player in the league? Hint: He is the only player who is also a grandfather.

Robert Parish
Bill Cartwright ■
Moses Malone ▲

This current coach (active in the 1994-95 season) has the record for the most consecutive 50-or-more-wins season. In 13 years of coaching, he has never fallen below the 50-win mark. Who is he?

Lenny Wilkens ●
Pat Riley
Larry Brown ▲

In Game 3 of the 1995 NBA Finals, Nick Anderson attempted a record number of three-pointers in a Finals contest. How many three-point shots did he attempt?

22 ●
16 ■
12 ▲

Which player holds the record for the most complete games played in one season? This player played the entire game 79 times out of a possible 80. The only time he did not play an entire game came when he was ejected for two technical fouls. Not once during the year did he come out because of foul trouble or injury or to rest.

Bill Russell ●
Wilt Chamberlain ■
Randy Smith ▲

Did you know that even though the NBA regular season is 82 games long, the record for the most games played in a season by one player is 88! In 1968-69, this player played 35 games with the New York Knicks before being traded to the Detroit Pistons. At the time, Detroit had only played 29 games, so when he played in each of the Pistons' final 53 games, he set a record for having played 88 regular season games. Who was he?

Dave DeBusschere ●
Willis Reed ■
Walt Bellamy ▲

Though the Boston Celtics have won more championships than any other team, they never once produced a league scoring champion. Who owns the team record as the franchise's top point producer?

Larry Bird
Kevin McHale
John Havlicek

Red Auerbach has guided a record nine championship teams. Who is the coach in second place with five title teams?

John Kundla
Tommy Heinsohn
Pat Riley

When a player is fouled attempting a three-pointer and the shot misses, he is awarded three free throws. If the three-pointer is made, then the shooter is awarded one free throw in addition to the three points, making for a possible four-point play if he can convert the free throw. Which player owns the record for the most four-point plays with 10?

Reggie Miller ●
Michael Adams ■
Steve Kerr ▲

Which player holds the record for the most minutes played in a Finals game?

Kevin Johnson
Garfield Heard
Jo Jo White

Eight steals in one game is often a good number for an entire team! But in a 1985 game, this guard set an all-time record with eight steals in one quarter. No ball was safe from this king of swipes. Who was he?

Lafayette "Fat" Lever
Alvin Robertson
Quinn Buckner

Who won the first NBA Slam-Dunk Championship in 1984?

Julius Erving
Clyde Drexler
Larry Nance

Who was the NBA's top dunker in the 1993-94 season with 381 jams?

Shawn Kemp
Chris Webber
Shaquille O'Neal

Who owns the record for most points (25) scored in one quarter of an NBA Finals game?

Michael Jordan ●
Isiah Thomas ■
Bob Pettit ▲

The Golden State Warriors set a record with the most three-pointers made in one game, in a winning effort against the Minnesota Timberwolves on April 12, 1995. How many threes did the Warriors net that night?

20 ●
17 ■
12 ▲

This player owns the top three assists performances in a Finals game. Who is he?

Magic Johnson
Isiah Thomas
Dennis Johnson ▲

Which team was the NBA's top defensive club in 1993-94? This team held opponents to a mere 91.5 points per game while permitting its opponents to make only 43.1% of their shots.

Cleveland Cavaliers
Houston Rockets
New York Knicks ▲

89

Which player has the record for the most career triple-doubles (achieving double figures in three statistical categories in one game)? The record is 137.

Michael Jordan ●
Larry Bird ■
Magic Johnson ▲

90

The record for the highest-scoring non-overtime game is 320 points. The Golden State Warriors defeated this team, 162-158, on November 2, 1990:

Portland Trail Blazers ●
Detroit Pistons ■
Denver Nuggets ▲

Only two players in history have won the NBA Rookie of the Year Award and the Most Valuable Player Award in the same season. Wilt Chamberlain is one of them. Who is the other?

Michael Jordan ●
Kareem Abdul-Jabbar ■
Wes Unseld ▲

Wilt Chamberlain holds the record for the most rebounds in an NBA game. How many rebounds did Chamberlain get?

55 ●
36 ■
44 ▲

Wilt Chamberlain also holds the top seven places in the record book for most rebounds in a season. Who holds the eighth position?

Moses Malone
Bill Russell
Dennis Rodman ▲

Offensive rebounds have been compiled since 1973-74, one season after Wilt Chamberlain retired. Who holds the record for the most offensive rebounds all-time?

Buck Williams ●
Robert Parish ■
Moses Malone ▲

Dikembe Mutombo set a record for the most blocked shots in a seven-game playoff series during the 1993-94 Playoffs. How many did Dikembe swat away to set the record?

38 ●
25 ■
46 ▲

The largest crowd ever to attend an NBA regular season game is 61,983. The Detroit Pistons played this team at the Pontiac Silverdome in Pontiac, MI, January 29, 1988, to set the record:

Boston Celtics ●
Chicago Bulls ■
Los Angeles Lakers ▲

Only four players have ever achieved a quadruple-double, reaching double figures in four statistical categories in one game. Nate Thurmond did it in 1974, Alvin Robertson in 1986 and Hakeem Olajuwon in 1990. Who was the fourth and most recent player to attain a quadruple-double?

> Larry Bird ●
> David Robinson ■
> Patrick Ewing ▲

Which player owns the record for the most three-pointers made (five) in one quarter of a playoff game, through the 1994 Playoffs?

> Reggie Miller ●
> John Starks ■
> John Paxson ▲

Hitting the 50-point mark in a game is a rare and notable accomplishment; most players never reach that mark. Behind Michael Jordan, who did it 34 times including playoff games, which active player has posted the most 50-point performances, with seven?

David Robinson ●
Tom Chambers ■
Dominique Wilkins ▲

Patrick Ewing of the New York Knicks set the record for most blocked shots in an NBA Finals series in 1994 against the Houston Rockets. How many shots did Ewing reject?

30 ●
36 ■
42 ▲